Shine On

200 Inspirational Quotes to Brighten
Your Day from My Heart to Yours

Kathleen Brady

ISBN 978-1-64569-759-6 (paperback)
ISBN 978-1-64569-760-2 (digital)

Christian Faith Publishing, Inc.
832 Park Avenue
Meadville, PA 16335
www.christianfaithpublishing.com

Printed in the United States of America

Special appreciation to my father, James Brady, my mother, Joan Brady, and my mentor that God has put in my life Catherine McAnally for always believing in me and encouraging me to follow my dreams. Most of all, to our heavenly Father for giving me the inspiration to write this.

" **S**ometimes life can be like a stick
of chewing gum—
It can stretch you to your limit,
but with God, your spirit can
never be broken."

Positive thinking is free.

Negative thinking can be very costly.

*A*lways do what is right, even
if you feel you are going the
wrong way.

We need to reach deep within so our life can truly begin.

*C*ompassion is one word, but it has a powerful impacting meaning.

When in an environment you feel uncomfortable, leave—it may be toxic.

Plug into positive energy that recharges you, not energy that drains you.

*I*n whose life today can you add a little brightness too.

Do you prefer your speed or God speed?

I prefer not to get a speeding ticket.

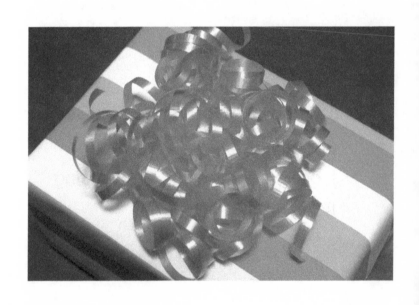

We all have been given a special gift in life. It is up to us to unwrap it and share it with the world.

*E*mpty hands are useless.

Serving hands are useful.

*Y*our emotions are contagious—
positive or negative.
Which one do you want to share
with people?

*T*here are great dreamers in life, but an achiever can make their dreams happen.

H earing is one thing, but listening is an art.

$\mathcal{S}$uccess is a seven-letter word, but its meaning is endless.

Work hard, play hard, but give your very best to our God.

Love is a short word, but its meaning is worldwide.

D ig deep within yourself and believe that you can do things that you want even if you do it afraid.

*B*e the ray of bright sunshine in someone's day.

$\mathcal{S}$omebody today needs your beautiful smile.

$\mathcal{S}$hine on with your inner light brightly, and it will naturally shine on the outside.

*B*e that shining light today for someone that may be in the darkness.

W e have two ears and one mouth. By giving your listening ear today to someone may just be the medicine they need for their soul.

*T*oday is all we have at this moment. Treasure it, live it to the fullest, and don't forget to tell all those how much you love them.

Sometimes it might seem a little bit difficult, but it is so much nicer to be selfless than selfish.

We are all capable of being
something bigger than ourself.

*E*veryone is given opportunities in life. It is a choice to recognize it and not let the right one pass you by.

*T*oday lead with love, joy, peace, kindness, goodness, faithfulness, gentleness, and self-control.

We all are offered opportunities in life, but there just may be an expiration date.

*A*re you a God pleaser or people pleaser?

Walk out the door today with your head held high. Remember, God does not make junk.

*1*s God in your driver's seat or passenger's seat of life?

G od created you to do great things. Borrow his belief in you when you don't believe in yourself.

We have a choice to become an encourager or discourager. Whose life can you give a little encouragement to?

A dream is just a word until it is put into action.

We are all meant to soar like an eagle.
Please don't let life or anyone clip your wings or hold you back.

Sometimes it may be a bit more challenging, but it is so much nicer to be selfless than selfish.

We all have the capability of being something bigger than ourself.

When encountering people today, greet them with kindness and a smile. You never know what they may be going through in their life. You could be the positive influence that they may need at that exact moment.

We will all encounter little hiccups in the road of life. But what will it really matter a week from now.

We can choose to be an encourager in life by inspiring, complimenting, smiling, and giving a kind word. Everyone wants to feel that they matter in life.

S elf-confidence begins with our mind. It is a very powerful tool. Don't let it tell you that you cannot do something or give you the feeling of self-doubt.

D ig deep within yourself and believe in you that you can do things even if you do them afraid. Once you get started, you may see your fear dissipate.

 L ife is like a rubber band. It can
stretch us to our limit, but with
God's will and guidance, we can
snap back.

Walk out the door today with your head held high. Remember, God does not make junk.

*I*s God in your driver's seat or passenger's seat of life?

*B*efore making a big decision in life, do an inner check on you.

*A*lways follow your heart, it will lead to a warm fuzzy place.

*1*f someone is toxic to you, don't stay and smell the fumes.

*y*ou have an emotional gas tank.
Are you running on empty or on
a full tank?

*P*eople can either deplete us or complete us.

When encountering difficult people, listen with respect, honor their opinion, and ponder the thought. If what seems to be true, maybe the issue could just be with you.

*P*eople can have the ability to empower us or enable us. I choose the first one.

L ife can be challenging at times. It is refreshing to be with someone who accepts you just the way you are. This is what I call a true friend.

F orever grateful

A ccepting

M emories in the making

I nspiring

L oving

Y our encourager.

You truly are so blessed!

*y*ou are one of a kind, different from the rest, use your gifts to become your very best.

*I*s negative draining you? Take time to plug in the drain and refill it with positivity.

*D*o you feel overloaded in life? It is time to unload, reload with lighter baggage. You will also save on gas.

Boundaries sometimes are a good thing in life. They may keep you away from the electric fence.

Do you hold a grudge or give people a nudge?

*I*ntuition is a gift from God. It can be like a traffic light. Go. Stop. Or proceed with caution.

G od can mend your broken heart
one stitch at a time.

*P*hysically and emotionally you need balance in your life. If you don't, you may be caught off guard.

*I*nner peace is like liquid gold, it flows with warmth and ease.

Life is like a revolving door. You will continue to go round and round, if you don't take a leap of faith and choose a path.

Sometimes life can give us a run for our money. They key is not to run, don't take the money, have faith, and don't take the bait.

Build people up and see how much they can grow.

S ometimes life can feel like you have a flat tire. You keep trying to move forward but don't seem to get anywhere.

Be humble and never take anything for granted in life. It can be taken away in a split second.

Kindness is a free gift to give to a stranger.

*Y*our smile could be the only
positive encouragement
someone receives today.

Remember to keep a life full of integrity. It may not always be easy but the benefits outweigh the disadvantages.

F ollow your heart, what is right, and true to you.

We can all be like a sparkling angel, adding a little sparkle and help changing one life at a time.

*L*ove is a universal word. Who today can you give a hug or share conversation with?

Sometimes things can be like pebble in your shoe. You have to shake it out and move on.

When somebody slams a door of opportunity in your face, go quietly and open a new one.

When you awake in the morning to start your day, just trust and have faith that things will be okay.

We all have choices in life to make. Some we may regret, but today is a new day, and we learn from our experiences. Today could be a brand-new beginning for you.

Sometimes we need to press forward even when we feel our emergency brake is on in life. We can surprise ourself what we can accomplish when we get out of our own way.

*L*ife can be like a sponge. It absorbs all the clutter of the world. We need to rinse out the sponge just like renewing our mind. Release the clutter so we can focus on what God has created us to do.

*P*hysically we may not be able to lift someone, but emotionally we can.

*H*ope is not lost. It just may be hiding, waiting for you to discover it.

I'd rather spread a little bit of kindness than a cold.

*H*ang on to hope tight. It will never let you go.

The antidote to being unhappy is
a smile.

*N*egative thinking is like a disease. It infects everyone you can come in contact with.

*N*egative thinking can be like a car spinning out of control. If you don't stop it, eventually it will self-destruct.

*N*o need to focus on fears and doubt. With God by your side, he will figure it out.

*I*f a cup of coffee can boost someone's energy, you have the energy to boost someone else's self-confidence.

*A*s the days of winter are getting darker, whose day can you make a little brighter?

*U*nfortunately, life did not come with a manual, but it did come with a book. It is called the Bible.

*T*he word rest is easy to say, but sometimes so hard to do.

A smile and a hello to a stranger may just be the beginning to a new friendship.

$\mathcal{W}$e need to first be a true friend
in order to have a true friend.

We may not have the means to be rich financially, but we do have the means to be rich spiritually.

*T*he antidote for stress is rest.

A dream is just a word until it is put into action.

We may be able to close our book of life to others, but with God, our book will always be open.

$y$ou will always be taking a risk with an airline pilot. But with God as your pilot, you will always be safe.

*A*s a bright star twinkles in the sky, remember you will always be the apple of God's eye.

A mechanic is skilled to fix your problems with a car. Allow God's power to fix your problems in life.

*P*eople will tend to dig a deep hole
in life. It is up to them to decide if
they want help filling it in.

*W*hen troubles knock at your door, tell them to go away because they are not welcome here.

God is our Good Shepherd. He will never lead you astray.

When God made you, he handpicked you, especially for me.

Don't be paralyzed in fear, allow
our Good Shepherd to steer.

Our Shepherd is steadfast, that is why we should never feel like an outcast.

With God, we lack nothing.

Without God, we gain nothing.

We can ponder and wander all we want, but we can choose to lift up our hands and ask God what does he want.

Do it again. Repeat.

Do it again. Repeat.

This is the only way we will have

victory over defeat.

G od is our Shepherd whether we are far or near. He will always have a listening ear.

$\mathcal{S}$ometimes when you feel totally alone, remember to rely on God. He will call you home.

Touch someone's life who may feel hopeless. It may be what they need to feel hopeful.

Just as we like to play in the sand,
always remember God will hold
your hand.

*B*elieve in yourself and remember
God is your partner, and he will
never leave you alone.

When you look at yourself in the mirror, make sure it is not fogged.

L ife can be like a pinball machine, randomly going up and down. Let God into your life and discover his love that can be found.

7f you are feeling down, bring yourself before the One who wears the crown.

*A*lways remember things will be okay because God's love will never go away.

When life throws you a curveball of stress, God wants your mind to truly rest.

*A*n angel's existence may be right around the corner; you never know how many you will encounter.

We never know where an angel
may be if we follow the light we
will truly see.

*H*ave you ever met a person with a sparkle in their eye? I can assure you that they are the apple of God's eyes.

Are you just giving lip service or
talking truly with a purpose?

*L*ife can be like a jigsaw puzzle;
we are constantly trying to find
where we fit in.

L ike going through a wandering maze, when you follow God's path, you will truly be amazed.

$y$ou may just be touching someone's heart even though you live miles apart.

When you feel like you are sinking
deep within, allow God to help
your life begin.

*Y*our faith can be like a dead battery. It just needs a jump start.

*y*our spirit can be like a gas tank, faithful or faithless. This is the only time running on less is truly more.

When you are truly feeling down and out, trust in God he will figure it out.

When you are in deep despair, lift up your hands to God in the air.

Remember, God will always wipe your tears because He is a God who can handle your fears.

When you are lonely and feel all alone, remember you can allow God's heart to be your home.

Our life can be extremely painful
at times, put your trust in God
and allow him to leave the pain
behind.

𝒴our heart may have a crack but
allow God to restore it back.

When you allow God to be your rock, there is no road that will be blocked.

*N*ever trust the GPS in your car, it just may lead your way too far. When you follow God's GPS, you will never have to call for an SOS.

Remember, when you are tucked
into bed tonight, God's hand will
hold you tight.

*I*f you allow God's spirit to lift you high, you have no idea how you will soar in the sky.

*I*f you allow God into your head, you cannot imagine how much your wings will spread.

*G*od gave us one heart. Tend to it with special care. So when it becomes fragile, God will be there.

When water continues to flow, we need God's help to let the hurt go.

*I*f your well is running dry, try God's well—his will never run dry.

Remember I love you, but God is truly the one to carry you though.

When life feels like a total mess,
reach out to God and truly
confess.

1 don't want earthly desires. Instead I choose what God desires.

*P*eople may let you down, but with God, you will never frown.

When you have problems in life,
turn them over to God, he will
always have a solution.

A material gift is nice, but the gift
of encouragement is priceless.

When you have lost a loved one and feel astray, remember in your heart they are not far away.

*W*hen you are feeling truly blue, remember God's love will always be with you.

When you have lost someone
close to your heart, remember
they are with God but not far
apart.

*D*o not let unhealthy distractions become your daily attractions in life.

*I*f you can stay steadfast to God and stay laser focus on his path that he made especially for you, you may just be surprised that your dreams may come true.

𝒴ou can get into trouble by listening the wrong way.

By fueling your mind, body, and soul, we need to be willing to let all the friction go.

Remember to recharge yourself daily and plug into God.

$\mathcal{W}$hen life seem like a merry-go-round, allow God in your life to settle you down.

*J*ust as your cell phone needs to be recharged, we need to recharge and renew our mind, body, and soul.

A heart is to be handled with special care. It is very fragile, so beware.

*I*t is not humans I want to impress. The only one I truly want to impress is God our heavenly Father.

We can give the gift of forgiveness to someone. It is a gift that is free and can be priceless to set you free.

*F*orgiveness can be a powerful gift to pass on so others can see.

Sometimes life can be like a snowdrift that piles high, all we can do is throw our hands to the sky.

*A*s you cast your fishing pole in the sea, you never know what will be at the end of line, but with God by your side, you know everything will be fine.

Beach Blessings

*I*n memory of my grandfather John "Jack" Cochran who loved the water.

*O*ur emotions are like waves of an ocean—they either go up and down or back and forth.

Do your emotions crash like a tidal wave? Or trickle like a stream?

*N*ever follow anyone's footprints
in the sand, but God's.

$\mathcal{W}$hen you follow other people's footprints in the sand, they can lead you in the wrong direction.

$\mathcal{J}$ ust like millions of unique grains of sand, we are all unique creation of God and have a special purpose in life.

When the stars shine off the glistening waters at night, we are to be like them—the light in the darkness.

A s the oceans crystal clear water is wide and deep, so is God's unconditional love for us.

*L*ike a gentle breeze on the beach, God's peacefulness can live in our hearts.

We are all like shells—we can either crawl in or crawl out of them.

*L*ike a shattered piece of glass, we may feel cracked, broken, and crushed, but in God's eyes, we are perfect, and our spirit can never be broken.

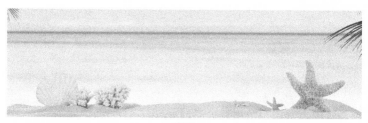

L ike a pearl is precious and safe in an oyster—we are always safe when we are in the hands of God.

When a seagull gets caught up in the turbulence of the wind, it can ride the current just like God will carry you through your trials and tribulations.

The beach is my happy place in life where I get nourishment for my soul.

A sand dollar has a story to tell,
do you know it?

A starfish needs help getting back into the ocean. Allow God to help you get your life back into order.

*A*n insult can be like a jellyfish when stepped on it stings.

We need to be free from fear so we can trust and realize God is near.

The beaches are one of God's great creations, made for us to enjoy and share with future generations.

*O*cean waves are God's music to calm our inner being.

Jellyfish are poisonous to the touch. What's in your life that may be poisonous to you?

There are a lot of predators in the ocean just like on land. The key is to trust your instinct when you sense danger.

G od is our ROCK!
Do you have a rock collection or
a pebble collection?

Sea glass becomes smooth over thousands of years tumbling in the ocean waters, be patient, gentle, and kind to yourself as you become the beautiful creation God created you to be.

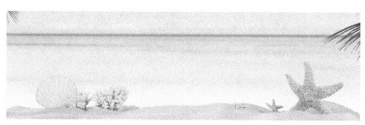

$\mathcal{J}$ust like what treasures the waves wash up to shore, we never know what amazing thing lies ahead of us in life in days to come.

*M*ay our love for each other in life
be as fluid as the ocean.

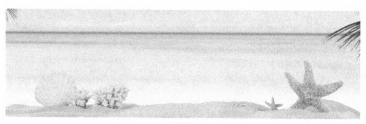

A s the waves roll continuously in
the ocean—God's love for us is
continuous and unconditional.

*D*rift wood has a tendency to wander aimlessly in the ocean. We have a God that does not want us to wander or drift apart from him.

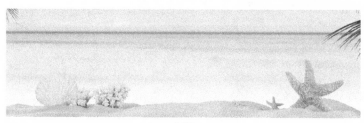

*A*nchors are for boats to keep them from going astray; God is our anchor in life to keep us close to him and from going away.

As the ocean water slams against the sharp cliffs, we are to be resilient like the water and bounce back.

A s God created the oceans and seas, may he bless you over the years to be.

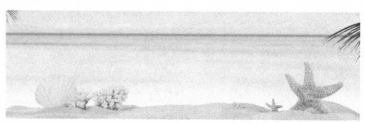

$\mathcal{J}$ust as the sand has a purpose at the beach—we all have a purpose to fulfill in life.

As you feel the warmth of the sand between your toes—may you feel the warmth of God in your heart.

As a star twinkles in the sky—
we are to be the twinkle in
someone's eye.

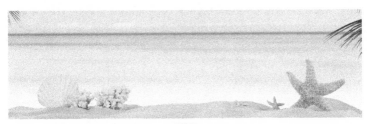

A boat needs a light to see in the darkness. We can be a light in the world for people to see.

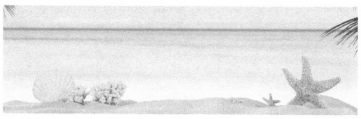

Saltwater is dangerous for us to drink—God has given us a gift of the "Spirit of the Living Water."

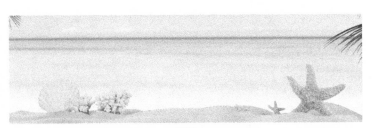

*M*ay your heart leave an everlasting impression of God's unconditional love in the sand.

God loves you.

About the Author

Kathleen Brady has accomplished many endeavors in her life. She is a mom to two furry children. She was an international bodybuilder, model, hairstylist, and entrepreneur. Her greatest passion in life is her love for people. She has always gravitated to positive quotes and inspirational books. She wrote this book to give hope, inspiration, and encouragement to add sparkle and to brighten your day!

CPSIA information can be obtained
at www.ICGtesting.com
Printed in the USA
LVHW031138040720
659733LV00002B/71